TOWER HAMLETS PUBLIC LIBRARY
C00120810

D0533696

Charles Dickens's

The Signalman

Peter Leigh

Published in association with The Basic Skills Agency

Hodder & Stoughton

A MEMBER OF THE HODDER HEADLINE GROUP

TOWER HAMLETS
LIBRARIES

HEA £3·99

1 8 MAR 2003

LOCN. | CLASS
Bow.D | J428.6

ACC. No.
CI208181

Acknowledgements
Cover: Matthew Williams
Illustrations: Jim Eldridge
Photograph of Charles Dickens © The Hulton Getty Picture Collection Limited

Orders: please contact Bookpoint Ltd, 39 Milton Park, Abingdon, Oxon OX14 4TD. Telephone: (44) 01235 400414, Fax: (44) 01235 400454. Lines are open from 9.00–6.00, Monday to Saturday, with a 24 hour message answering service. Email address: orders@bookpoint.co.uk

British Library Cataloguing in Publication Data
A catalogue record for this title is available from The British Library

ISBN 0 340 74309 3

First published 1999
Impression number 10 9 8 7 6 5 4 3 2 1
Year   2005 2004 2003 2002 2001 2000 1999

Copyright © 1999 Peter Leigh

All rights reserved. No part of this publication may be reproduced or transmitted in any form or by any means, electronic or mechanical, including photocopy, recording, or any information storage and retrieval system, without permission in writing from the publisher or under licence from the Copyright Licensing Agency Limited. Further details of such licences (for reprographic reproduction) may be obtained from the Copyright Licensing Agency Limited, of 90 Tottenham Court Road, London W1P 9HE.

Typeset by Fakenham Photosetting Ltd, Fakenham, Norfolk.
Printed in Great Britain for Hodder & Stoughton Educational, a division of Hodder Headline Plc, 338 Euston Road, London NW1 3BH by Redwood Books, Trowbridge, Wiltshire.

About the author

Charles Dickens was born in 1812
and died in 1870.
He is one of our most popular writers.

About the story

TOWER
HAMLETS
LIBRARY

This story is set
in the early days of railways,
when the trains ran on steam.

There were no computers then,
everything had to be done by hand.
The signalmen were very
important workers on the railway.
They sent and received signals
telling them whether the line
was clear or not,
and they told the trains
whether they could go or stop.

They often lived lonely lives
in remote parts of the country.

'Hello! Below there!'

When he heard my voice calling to him,
he was standing at the door of his box,
with a flag in his hand.

The signalman's **box**
is by the railway line
near the entrance
of a tunnel.
The story-teller
is on the hill
above him.

I would have thought
that he must have known
from where my voice came.

But instead of looking up to where I stood
on the top of the cutting
nearly over his head,
he turned himself around,
and looked down the Line.

The **cutting**
is where the rock
has been removed
at the entrance
of the tunnel.

something very
strange about the
way that he did it

There was something very strange
in his manner of doing so,
though I couldn't for the life of me
say what it was.

1

'Hello! Below!'

From looking down the Line,
he turned himself around again,
and, raising his eyes,
saw me high above him.

'Is there any path
by which I can come down
and speak to you?'

He looked up at me
without saying anything.

Just then there came a soft vibration
in the earth and air,
quickly changing
into a violent throbbing.
A train rushed out of the tunnel.
It made me jump back
from the edge of the cutting.

When the smoke had cleared
I looked down again,
and saw him putting away his flag.
I repeated my question.

After a pause,
during which he watched me carefully,
he pointed to a place
two or three hundred yards away.

I called down to him, 'All right!'
and made for that point.
There was a rough zigzag path there
which I followed down.

clammy – very damp

The cutting was very deep
and very steep.
It was made through clammy stone
that became oozier and wetter
as I went down.

He watched me very carefully
all the way down the path
and up the Line
to where he was standing.

'This must be a lonely job,' I said.

He said nothing, but turned
and looked strangely
towards the red light
at the mouth of the tunnel,
and looked all about it,
and then looked at me.

'You're in charge of the light as well?'
I asked.

He answered in a low voice,
'Don't you know I am?'

spirit – ghost

He looked as though he were a spirit,
not a man.

'You look at me,'
I said, forcing a smile,
'as if you were afraid of me.'

'I wasn't sure,' he said,
'if I had seen you before.'

'Where?'
He pointed to the red light.

'There?' I said.

'Yes!'

'My good fellow, what should I do there?
I was never there, you may be sure.'

'Yes,' he said, 'I think I may.
Yes, I am sure I may.'

They both relaxed.

with readiness
– eagerly

His manner cleared, like my own.
He replied to my remarks with readiness,
and in well-chosen words.

Lots of people
depended on him
but he didn't have
much hard work.

Had he much to do there?
Yes – he had enough responsibility,
but not much actual work.

Was it a lonely life?
Yes – but he had grown used to it.

Did he have to stay down here
all the time
in this dark, damp cutting?
Sometimes, when the Line wasn't busy,
he came up, but not for long.

telegraph – the
first electronic
communication,
using Morse Code

He took me into his hut,
where there was a fire,
a desk, and a telegraph.
He told me more of his life.
He had been a student,
and had attended lectures.
But he had run wild,
and wasted his opportunities.

The signalman thinks
it is too late
to change his life.

He did not complain.
He had made his bed,
and he lay upon it.
It was far too late to make another.

He spoke in a quiet manner,
and called me 'sir.'
Except that as he was speaking,
he twice broke off,
opened the door of the hut,
and looked out towards the red light
at the mouth of the tunnel.

Both times he came back to the fire
with the same strange look he had
when I first saw him.

contented – happy

I said, 'You almost make me think
that I have met with a contented man.'

'I believe I used to be so,'
he said in his low voice,
'but I am troubled, sir,
I am troubled.'

'With what?
What is your trouble?'

'It is very difficult to say, sir.
It is very, very difficult to speak of . . .
What made you cry,
"Hello! Below there!" tonight?'

'Heaven knows,' I said.
'I cried something like that –'

'Not *like* that, sir.
Those were the very words.
I know them well.'

'I admit those were the very words.
I said them, no doubt,
because I saw you below.'

'For no other reason?'

'What other reason
could I possibly have?'

'You had no feeling
that they were sent to you
in any supernatural way?'

**in any supernatural
way** – by a ghost

'No!'

He paused.
'I took you for someone else
this evening. That troubles me.'

'That mistake?'

'No. That someone else.'

'Who is it?'

'I don't know.'

'Like me?'

'I don't know.
I never saw the face.
The left arm is across the face,
and the right arm is waved – this way.'

He showed me.
It was the action
of someone shouting

**with the utmost
passion** – as if his
life depended on it

with the utmost passion,
'For God's sake, clear the way!'

He carried on.

'One moonlight night,' he said,
I was sitting here, when I heard a voice cry,
"Hello! Below there!"

I started up –
I jumped up

I started up,
looked from that door,
and saw this someone else
standing by the red light
near the tunnel,
waving just as I showed you.

'The voice seemed hoarse with shouting,
and it cried, "Look out! Look out!"
And then again,
"Hello! Below there! Look out!"

'I caught up my lamp,
turned it on red,
and ran towards the figure, calling,
"What's wrong?
What has happened?
Where?"
'The figure stood just outside the tunnel.
It still had its arm across its face.
I ran right up to it,
and had my hand stretched out
to pull the arm away,
when it was gone.'

'Into the tunnel?' I said.

'No. I ran into the tunnel,
five hundred yards.
I stopped,
and held my lamp above my head.
All I saw were the wet stains
dripping down the walls.
I ran out again
faster than I had run in.
I looked all around the red light
with my own red light,
and then I ran back here.

'I telegraphed both ways.
"An alarm has been given.
Is anything wrong?"

'The answer came back, both ways,
"All well."'

I felt as if a frozen finger
was slowly tracing down my spine.
'It must be imagination,' I said.
'It must be . . .'

He touched my arm.

'I have not finished,' he said.
'Within six hours,
there was a great accident on this Line.
Within ten hours,
the dead and wounded
were brought through the tunnel
to the very spot
where the figure had stood.'

Another shudder crept over me.
I tried to stop it,
and to say that this was coincidence,
but he lay his hand on my arm again
and said that he still had not finished.

coincidence –
chance

'This,' he said, 'was just a year ago.
Six or seven months passed,
and I had recovered from the shock.
One morning, I was standing at the door.
I looked towards the red light,
and I saw the ghost again.'

He stopped and stared at me.

'Did it cry out?' I asked.

'No. It was silent.'

'Did it wave its arm?'

'No. It leaned against the light
with both hands in front of its face.
Like this.'

He showed me again.

mourning – sorrow
for the dead

It was like someone in mourning.
I have seen such figures
carved on tombstones.

'Did you go up to it?'

'I came in and sat down,
partly to collect my thoughts,
and partly because it had
turned me faint.
When I went to the door again,
the ghost was gone.'

'But nothing followed?
Nothing came of this?'

He touched me on the arm
with his forefinger twice or thrice,
ghastly – death-like   giving a ghastly nod each time.

'That very day,
as a train came out of the tunnel,
I saw people waving and shouting at me
from a window on my side.
In those days there
were no corridors
on the trains,
so you could not
get to the driver.
Only the signalman
outside could tell
him to stop.

I saw them just in time
to signal to the driver, Stop!
He shut off,
and put his brake on,
but the train drifted past here
a hundred and fifty yards or more.

'I ran after it,
and, as I went along,
heard terrible screams and cries.
A beautiful young lady had died suddenly
in one of the compartments.
She was brought in here,
and laid down on this floor between us.'

I couldn't help but push my chair back,
and look at the boards
at which he pointed.

'True, sir. True.
Just as it happened,
so I tell you.'

I could think of nothing to say,
and my mouth was dry.
The wind wailed
through the wires outside.

wires – telegraph
wires

He carried on. 'Now, sir, mark this,
and judge how my mind is troubled.
The ghost came back a week ago.
Ever since it has been there,
now and again, by fits and starts.'

'At the light?'

'At the light.'

'What does it seem to do?'

He showed me, with even more passion,
the same action of
'For God's sake, clear the way!'

He went on,
'I have no peace or rest for it.
It calls to me,
for many minutes together,
in an agonised voice,
"Below there! Look out! Look out!"
It stands waving to me. It . . .'

agonised – pained

'Did it come earlier,
when I was here,
and you went to the door?'

'Twice!'

'And did the ghost seem to be there,
when you looked out?'

'It *was* there.'

'Both times?'

'Both times!'

'Will you come to the door with me,
and look for it now?'

He bit his lip,
as though he did not want to,
but arose.

I opened the door,
and stood on the step,
while he stood in the doorway.

'Do you see it?' I asked.

'No,' he answered. 'It is not there.'

'Agreed,' I said.

We went in again,
shut the door,
and sat down back in our seats.

'What troubles me so dreadfully,'
he said, 'is what does the ghost mean?'

I said I didn't understand him.
'What is it warning against?'
he said, staring into the fire.
'What is the danger?
Where is the danger?
There *is* danger waiting
somewhere on the Line.

calamity – disaster

Some dreadful calamity *will* happen.
It is not to be doubted this third time,
after what has gone before.
But surely this is a cruel haunting of *me*.
What can *I* do?'

He pulled out his handkerchief,
and wiped the drops from his heated
forehead.

'If I telegraph Danger,
on either side of me, or on both,
I can give no reason for it.
I should get into trouble,
and do no good.
This is what would happen:
Message: "Danger! Take care!"
Answer: "What danger? Where?"
Message: "Don't know.
But for God's sake, take care!"
They would sack me.
What else could they do?'

His pain of mind was sad to see.
He was a conscientious man,
worried by a possible danger to life
that he could do nothing about.

conscientious –
obeying your
conscience, always
doing what you
have to do

'When it first stood under the light,'
he went on, 'why didn't it tell me
where that accident was to happen –
if it must happen?
Why not tell me
how it could be prevented –
if it could have been prevented?
When on its second coming
it hid its face,
why didn't it tell me,
"She is going to die.
Let them keep her at home"?
If it came on those two times,
just to show me
that its warnings were true,
and so prepare me for the third,
why not warn me plainly now?
And why me? A poor signalman.
Why not go to someone higher up
with more power to act?'

When I saw him in this state,
I felt I had to calm his mind,
both for his sake,
and for the safety of the passengers.

We talked on,
and he became calmer.
I left him at two in the morning.
I offered to stay through the night,
but he would not hear of it.

He had a change of duty the next night.
I agreed to come back at that time.
I said I would go with him to a doctor,
and get his advice.

Next evening was a lovely evening,
and I walked out early to enjoy it.

The sun was not quite down
when I came to the top of the cutting.

I cannot describe my feelings
when I saw a man
at the mouth of the tunnel.
He had his left arm over his face,
and was waving his right arm.

The horror that gripped me
passed in a moment.
For I saw that it really was a man,
and that there was a group
of other men nearby,
to whom he seemed
to be demonstrating the gesture.
There was a sheet on the ground
next to them.

demonstrating –
showing, describing

With a sense that something was wrong,
and that it was my fault
for leaving the signalman there alone,
I went down the path
as quickly as I could.

'What is the matter?' I asked the men.

'Signalman killed this morning, sir.'

'Not the man belonging to that box?'

'Yes, sir.'

'Not the man I know?'

'You will recognise him, sir,
if you knew him,' said one of the men,
and carefully raised one end
of the sheet,
'for his face is quite calm.'

'Oh, how did this happen,
how did this happen?' I asked.

'He was cut down by an engine, sir.
No man in England knew his work better.
But somehow
he was not clear of the outer rail.

It was just at broad day.
He had lit the light,
and had the lamp in his hand.
As the engine came out of the tunnel,
his back was towards her,
and she cut him down.

That man drove her,
and was showing how it happened.
Show the gentleman, Tom.'

The man stepped back
to the mouth of the tunnel.

Like a ship, an
engine is called
'she'.

25

check speed –
slow down and stop

take heed – take
notice

'Coming round the curve
in the tunnel, sir,' he said,
'I saw him at the end,
like through a telescope.
There was no time to check speed,
and I knew him to be very careful.
He didn't seem
to take heed of the whistle,
so I called to him as loud as I could.'

'What did you say?'

'I said, "Hello! Below there!
Look out! Look out!
For God's sake clear the way!"'

I started.

TOWER
HAMLETS
LIBRARY

'Ah! it was a dreadful time, sir.
I never left off calling to him.
I put this arm before my eyes
so as not to see,
and I waved this arm to the last,
but it was no use.'

There is no more to tell,
except to point out
that it was not only the same waving,
but also the very same words,
that had haunted the poor signalman.